ABOUT
SPACE AND STARS

Questions Kids Ask . . . about SPACE and STARS

continued

How many stars are there?

If you want to see the stars really well, you need to go far away from city lights and look up on a clear night. How many do you see?

You will have a hard time counting. Astronomers say that we can see up to about four thousand stars without a telescope. With a large telescope you might be able to see one billion stars if you traveled around the world.

But beyond that there may be a billion billion stars. No one has ever been able to count them all.

Where does space end?

Scientists and astronomers believe that space is an enclosed area. Although it is not round, space is much like the inside of a beach ball. Therefore, we could not travel outside of space if we wanted to.

Space begins where Earth's atmosphere ends, about 160 kilometres (100 miles) above the Earth's surface. As for where space actually ends—to get some idea of the possibilities, picture this:

Earth and other planets circle the sun;

beyond the farthest planet are the billions of other stars that make up our galaxy, the Milky Way;

now, beyond that, so astronomers believe, there are billions of other galaxies whirling through space.

What? You can't picture it? Don't feel bad. Such vastness is nearly impossible to imagine—and it is impossible to measure. So while scientists think that there is a limit to space, there is no way of knowing where it is.

THE BLACK HOLE

Why do stars twinkle?

When light reaches us from the distant stars, it has to pass through the envelope of air that surrounds us here on Earth. No matter how big a star is, and no matter where you stand, you can never see more of a star with the naked eye than a pinpoint of flickering light in the sky. Why? Stars are very far away—the closest star to us is more than 50 *trillion* kilometres (30 trillion miles) away. Because the stars are so far away, their light is only the tiniest beam when it reaches Earth, and that thin beam is easily scattered by the air it has to pass through.

DID YOU KNOW . . . planets do not twinkle. The reason is that they are closer and their reflected light has a thicker beam that is not so easily scattered by the air.

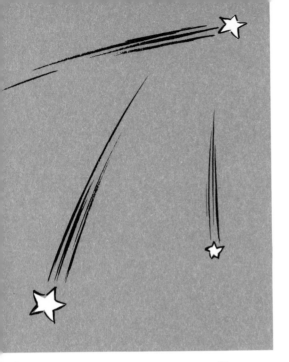

How fast do stars move?

If you watch the night sky for a few hours, you will note that the stars seem to move across it. However, they always keep to the same pattern. As you might have guessed, what is really happening is that the earth is spinning so that our position in relation to the stars changes.

In fact, the stars really are moving too. They may be speeding along at 10 kilometres (6 miles) per second. But because they are so far away it will take years and years before we can notice any change in their position.

Are all stars the same color?

Although we think of stars as white, the stars are many colors. There are blue, white, yellow, orange and red stars. The color depends on the heat of the star at its surface.

A red star has a surface temperature of about 2800°C (5000°F), and a blue star is ten times as hot. The sun, which is also a star, is about 5500°C (10 000°F). What color is the sun? You guessed it—it's a yellow star.

Stars have different temperatures because they are made up of different chemicals. Stars that are made mostly of gases—the blue ones—are the hottest. If there are metal particles in the star, they cool it down. The coolest stars are the ones that contain the most metal particles—the red ones.

How big are stars?

Many stars are about the same size as our star—the one we call the sun. It is called a dwarf star but it is not particularly small. In fact, our sun has a diameter 100 times bigger than the diameter of our Earth!

When stars get older, they seem to spread out like thin, hot vapor. These huge old stars shine very brightly. They are called red giants. Some stars may even become supergiants.

When stars are even older, they throw off their outer layers and become smaller and dimmer. These old stars are called white dwarfs.

What is the difference between a nova and a supernova?

The old, weak stars that are called white dwarfs move around other stars. Bits of matter from the other stars can fall on the white dwarfs and cause a reaction that makes the white dwarf shine brilliantly. It is then called a nova.

If even more matter falls on the star, it may collapse and burn. This star only lasts for a short time, but it shines very brilliantly while it lasts and is called a supernova.

What kind of vehicle do you need to drive on the moon?

The typical family car would not work at all on the moon! A moon vehicle needs to be powered by electrical batteries and it must also be strong enough to go over very rough ground.

The American space team developed something called a Lunar Roving Vehicle. It looks rather like a dune buggy, with four wheels and no roof. It can go 12 kilometres (7-1/2 miles) per hour and can carry lots of scientific equipment and several cameras. In spite of that, it is very light—weighing less than 200 kilograms (440 pounds).

The Soviets also invented a space vehicle called the Lunokhod 1. It looks like a giant old-fashioned bathtub on eight wheels. A lunokhod is rather like a robot, and one spent a whole year on the moon doing tests. It was operated by remote control from Earth.

What do astronauts wear in space?

When they are in their space craft, astronauts can wear comfortable clothing similar to what you might wear for jogging. If they go outside the craft, however, they have to wear clothing that is like a portable space craft. A typical spacesuit has tubes of water running through it to keep the astronaut at the right temperature. It has an outer layer that shields the wearer from radiation and extremes of temperature. In space, temperatures can range from 120°C (248°F) in the sun to −150°C (−238°F) in the shade.

Astronauts also need to take air with them, and they carry communication equipment so they can speak to other astronauts left in the spaceship or space scientists back on Earth.

The spacesuit would be bulky on Earth, but the lack of gravity in space allows the astronaut to wear all the heavy gear without feeling much of its weight.

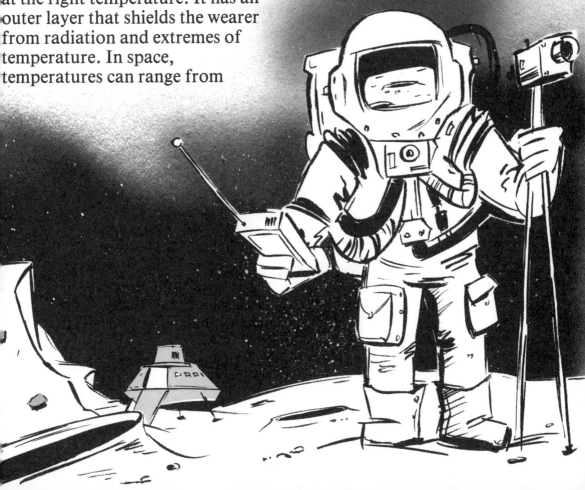

What would it be like to walk on the moon?

The force of gravity keeps your feet on the ground when you walk on the Earth. Gravity is the force that pulls two objects together. The moon does have its own gravity but it is much weaker than the Earth's because the moon is smaller. Everything is only one-sixth as heavy on the moon as it is on Earth. As a result, if people tried to walk on the moon, gravity would not pull their feet back down so strongly. They might find themselves taking a giant leap in slow motion every time they took a step.

DID YOU KNOW . . . the moon has no air because its gravity isn't strong enough to hold any close to its surface.

What is space junk and how much is there in space?

According to NORAD, the North American Aerospace Defense Command, there were about 5000 objects in orbit around the Earth in 1985.

Four out of five of these objects are not proper satellites at all. They are bits of "space junk" such as empty rocket cases and nose cones which accompanied satellites into space.

Of the proper satellites orbiting in 1985, less than 300 were operating. The ones which were not working might have wandered off course, or their electronic system might have failed.

Some objects fall naturally to Earth when they come close enough to be pulled down by Earth's gravity. When they enter the atmosphere, the friction with the air causes them to burn up. However, some pieces of space junk may not burn up completely. They may drop to the Earth's surface. As far as we know, only one death has been caused by space junk landing on Earth—that of a cow in Cuba.

How big is the moon?

The moon has a diameter of about 3480 kilometres (2160 miles). That measurement is only a quarter of the diameter of the Earth.

The rock that makes up the moon is not as dense as the rock that makes up the Earth. This means that a chunk of moon rock weighs less than a chunk of Earth rock, even though it is the same size.

Scientists calculate that the big, dense Earth weighs 81 times more than our little moon.

How does the moon move?

The moon is rather like a baby planet that belongs to the parent Earth. It travels in a circular orbit around the Earth, not the sun.

Remember, though, that the moon does stay with the Earth as the Earth travels around the sun.

The force of gravity that holds our moon close to the Earth holds it so tightly that the moon cannot spin. We only ever see one side of the moon from the Earth. It was not until people could travel in a spaceship that anyone had ever seen the "dark" side of the moon.

DID YOU KNOW . . . Mars and Neptune each have two moons, Uranus has five moons, Saturn has 10, and Jupiter has at least 12!

Are there any Martians on Mars?

If you ever took a trip to Mars to find out what it is like, you would have to take nearly everything you needed to survive with you. The air on Mars doesn't contain enough oxygen for you to breathe and there is no water to drink. The red soil sometimes blows around in violent dust storms.

You would have to explore deep canyons and huge round craters of long-dead volcanoes to look for Martians. There are huge ice fields at the poles.

Is there life on Mars? No one has discovered any yet . . . but who knows?

DID YOU KNOW . . . the large known mountain in the solar sys is on Mars. It is nearly three tim high as Mount Everest.

What is the Earth's address in space?

When you send a letter, you give the number of the house, the street name and the city or town. If you had to send a letter to the Earth from a far point in space, you might address it like this:

> Earth
> 3, Solar System
> Milky Way

The Earth is a ball of rock called a planet that travels around the sun in a circular path known as an orbit. There are two planets that are closer to the sun, which is why you would call Earth number three. Six more planets are further away. The sun and the nine planets are called the solar system. But the sun is just one of millions of stars in a group, or galaxy, called the Milky Way. The Milky Way is one of many galaxies that exist in the entire universe.

What causes an eclipse?

A solar eclipse occurs when the moon, orbiting the Earth, comes between the Earth and the sun. The moon blocks out the sun's light and casts a shadow on part of the Earth. Even though the moon is smaller than the sun, it can block out the sun's light. Because the sun is so far away, it appears to be about the same size as the moon.

A total eclipse begins slowly as the moon appears to cover the sun. The sky darkens and it looks as if something is taking bigger and bigger bites out of the sun. Finally it disappears altogether leaving a shining halo of light.

To understand how an eclipse works, try this experiment. You need a flashlight and a friend.

The flashlight is the sun. Place the flashlight somewhere so you can see it easily. Now stand about 6 metres (20 feet) away. Turn around slowly. You are pretending to be the Earth spinning around. As you do so, have your friend walk around you, about an arm's length away. Your friend is like the moon, orbiting the earth.

From time to time, your friend will come between you and the sun and block its light.

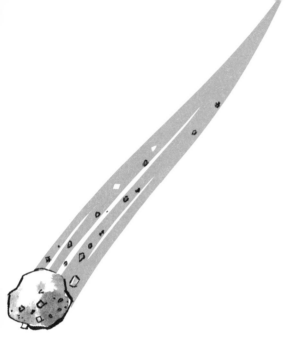

What causes the northern lights?

Have you ever looked up into the sky at night and seen curtains of green light hanging down from the sky? If you have, then you have seen the northern lights. They are sometimes called the *aurora borealis.*

The Inuit people once believed that the northern lights were reflections from the dance fires of ghosts. Now we know that the sun often throws "solar flares," which means that billions of tiny particles fly through space. These particles are electrically charged, and any that come near the North Pole are pulled towards it because of magnetism. The particles then mingle with the air. The oxygen in the air glows green as a result of this mingling.

The best times to see the northern lights are during March and September.

What are comets?

Comets are rather like huge, dirty snowballs in space. They consist of ice, bits of rock and gases.

Comets follow a regular orbit around the sun. Most of the time they are far beyond the farthest planet, but sometimes their orbit brings them sweeping close to earth. When they are near the sun, the heat makes them change shape and they develop a brilliant tail made of gas and dust.

DID YOU KNOW . . . Halley's comet has come close to Earth several times. It last appeared in 1986.

How fast do rockets fly?

In order to escape from the pull of gravity, rockets have to reach a speed of 28 000 kilometres (17 400 miles) per hour.

Rockets work in the same way as a balloon that you let go so the air can escape. The balloon whizzes all over the place as the air rushes out behind! Rocket engines also shoot air out behind the rocket. They are arranged one behind another on a space craft so that the back engines can help the ones in front. Once the engine has burned all its fuel, it is designed to fall away from the space craft. The craft gets lighter and can speed away.

What are satellites?

Satellite is the word for something that orbits a planet. All the moons are natural satellites. The Earth also has artificial satellites that have been taken into space by a rocket and set free to orbit the Earth. There are hundreds of satellites traveling around the Earth right now. They run on batteries powered by the sun and are controlled from Earth.

Satellites are used for different purposes. Some transmit radio and television programs. Others take photographs that may be used to help make maps, predict the weather, or spy on people. Some even have cameras that are strong enough to read licence plates of cars on city streets!

DID YOU KNOW . . . the Earth's first artificial satellite, Sputnik 1, was sent up by the Soviets in 1957.

21

Is there air in space?

The Earth is more than just dirt, rock and water. A very important part of the Earth is the atmosphere: the air we breathe. Air is a combination of gases, including oxygen, that forms a layer around the Earth.

The air stays with the Earth for the same reason that you don't float away. It is held here by gravity. Gravity is a force that very large objects have which attracts other objects to them. This is something like magnetism. You can take a magnet and use it to pick up a paper clip just by holding the magnet near it. Anything that gets close enough to the Earth will be held by it in much the same way.

Space is the area between the planets and the stars. There is no air in space because all gases are held by gravity to one or another of the planets or stars.

Because gravity is stronger at ground level than it is farther away, there is more air close to the ground. You can find a very little bit of air as far away from the Earth as 160 kilometres (100 miles), but as close as 10 kilometres (6 miles) up, there is already not enough air for us to be able to breathe.

Why does the moon seem to change shape?

When someone is sitting next to you, you can see the side of that person's face, with the nose and chin jutting out. When that person sits opposite you, you can see a full, round face.

The moon circles the Earth once every 28 days. When it is on the "side" of our part of the Earth, we can see a side view of the part of the moon that is in sunlight as a thin crescent. When it is opposite our part of the

Earth, we can see its full, round shape. When it moves to the other side, we see a side view again. Only this time the crescent points the other way. Of course, when it is behind our part of the Earth, we don't see it at all!

The first, thin crescent is called a new moon. The round moon is called the full moon. The second crescent is called the old moon. Then there is no moon for a few days, until we have a new moon again.

DID YOU KNOW . . . when the moon is getting bigger, it is called a waxing moon; when it is getting smaller, it is called a waning moon.

How hot is the sun?

If you stay out too long on a hot summer's day, you know that you risk getting burned. Imagine: the sun can burn you even though it is 150 million kilometres (93 million miles) away! How hot do you think it is on the sun?

Scientists can't get close enough to take the temperature with a thermometer. Instead they use clever mathematics to give them an idea of how hot the sun is. They think that the temperature at the center of the sun is about 15 000 000°C (27 000 000°F). The outside of the sun is cooler—about 5500°C (10 000°F).

At these temperatures, everything you can think of that exists on Earth would be burned up in no time. Suntan lotion wouldn't help a bit!

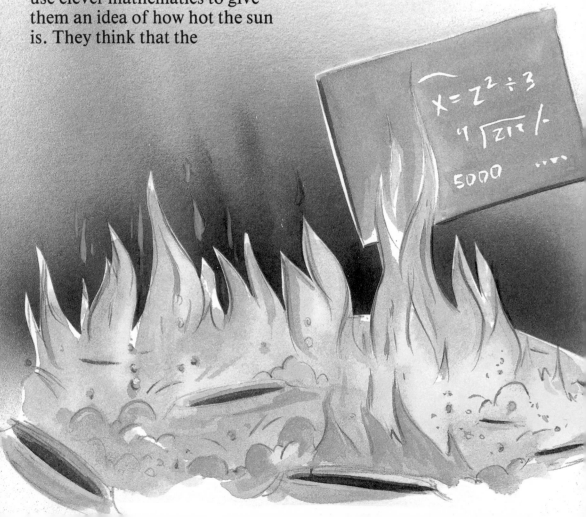

What is a sun dog?

If you look towards the sun on one of those days when the sky has a high ceiling of thin, even clouds, you might see a pale halo around the sun. On that halo you might notice two bright spots with white tails pointing away from the sun. These spots are called sun dogs. Sun dogs appear when ice crystals that float around in clouds bend the light from the sun in a special way.

The light from the moon can also be bent in the same way. The result is moon dogs.

What are sunspots?

Sunspots are dark spots that can be seen on the surface of the sun. What happens is that magnetic fields build up inside the sun. These magnetic fields actually hold the heat inside the sun and do not allow it to reach the surface. The result is that the patches of sun above these fields cool down a little. Because they are cooler than surrounding areas, they appear darker. A sunspot can be up to 30 000 kilometres (19 000 miles) in diameter.

DID YOU KNOW . . . some people have mistaken moon dogs for flying saucers!

25

Which planet is the biggest?

The largest planet in our solar system is called Jupiter. It was named after the king of the Roman gods. It is the fifth planet away from the sun and is 628 760 000 kilometres (390 700 000 miles) away from the Earth.

Jupiter is a huge ball of gas. It has a diameter of 142 000 kilometres (88 240 miles), 11 times larger than the diameter of the Earth.

A year on Jupiter lasts 4333 days, as that is the time it takes for the planet to orbit the sun. It is always very cold there—about $-150°C$ ($-238°F$).

Which planet is the smallest?

The smallest planet in the solar system is Pluto, named after the Roman god of the underworld. It is also the farthest away from the sun. That means that it is very far away from the Earth too— 5 765 500 000 kilometres (3 583 000 000 miles). In fact, no one knew that Pluto existed until 1930. Even now, people don't know very much about Pluto.

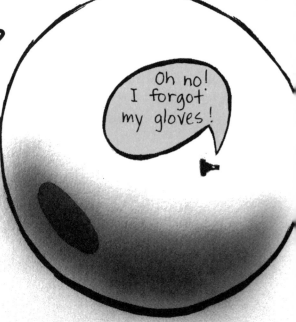

Why do some planets have rings?

No one knows exactly why three planets in our solar system—Saturn, Uranus and Jupiter—have rings. These planets are known as "Gas Giants" because they are made mostly of gases. They probably have small solid cores of rock and ice but are much lighter and less solid than the other planets with no rings.

Saturn has more than 100 rings. Viewed through a telescope, Saturn is one of the most spectacular sights in the night sky. Its rings are made up of billions of ice-covered particles of sand, grit and small stones. This "space junk" revolves around the planet in thin narrow rings.

The rings of Uranus can't even be seen through a telescope and were only discovered by accident in 1977. Astronomers believe these nine, narrow dark rings are made of larger boulders.

Jupiter's ring was discovered in 1979 as a result of a photograph taken by the Voyager I. It is too faint to be seen from Earth. The ring is made up of small particles.

What would happen if the Earth stopped spinning?

If the Earth stopped spinning, everything, as we know it, would change. If you were unlucky enough to be living on the side that faced away from the sun, your world would always be completely dark and very cold once the Earth stopped spinning. It would be like living in the Arctic winter all the time.

But if you lived on the sunny side, things wouldn't be much better. Without any darkness, most plants and animals would soon die because they need the dark of the night as much as daylight, to survive. Food would become very scarce and water would start evaporating under the scorching rays of the sun. Our climate would change drastically. Even if we survived all this, we would have no way to measure time and without time our

civilization would soon collapse.

Every planet in our solar
system is spinning. They are
moving around the sun as they
spin on their own axes like tops.
If Earth or any one of the planets
stopped spinning, it would mean
that the whole system was
breaking down.

Fortunately, chances of this
happening are very slim.

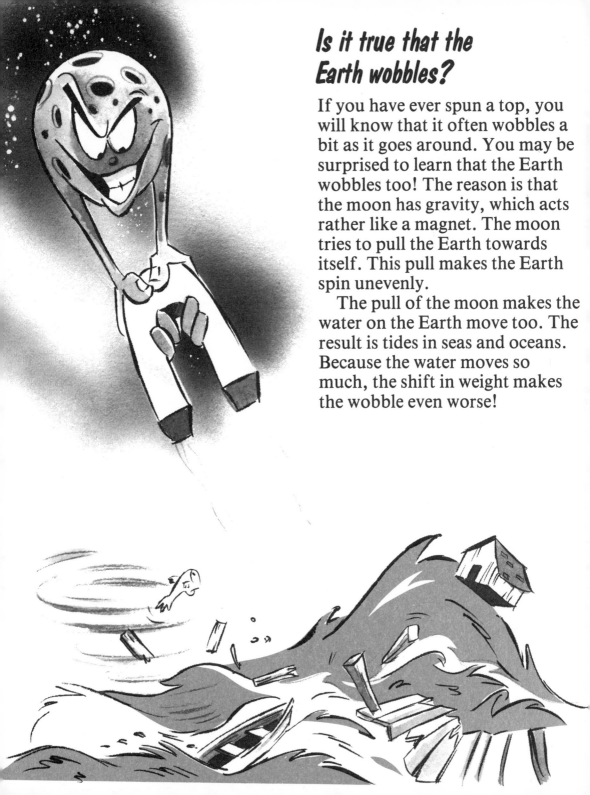

Is it true that the Earth wobbles?

If you have ever spun a top, you will know that it often wobbles a bit as it goes around. You may be surprised to learn that the Earth wobbles too! The reason is that the moon has gravity, which acts rather like a magnet. The moon tries to pull the Earth towards itself. This pull makes the Earth spin unevenly.

The pull of the moon makes the water on the Earth move too. The result is tides in seas and oceans. Because the water moves so much, the shift in weight makes the wobble even worse!

How does a space craft stay in orbit?

Once boosted out of the Earth's atmosphere and away from the force of Earth's gravity, a space craft could float without any direction.

To stop this from happening, special thruster rockets in the tail of the craft are set off at intervals to direct the craft on its way. Once a rocket has been used, it cannot be used again—rather like firework rockets! The astronauts need to have a good supply so they can steer their craft throughout its journey and then bring it back to Earth.

's orbiting the same s spinning?

Orbiting and spinning are two different types of movement. The Earth's orbit is the long journey it makes in a huge circle around the sun. At the same time as it travels along, the Earth also spins around like a top. It spins once around every 24 hours. When our part of the Earth is facing the sun, it is daytime for us. Then as the Earth spins further round the sun appears to sink down in the sky.

Of course, when we are in the light, the other side of the world is in darkness; when we are in the dark, the other side of the world is in light.

Index